ω 6/09 ω 9/12

OUR GALAXY AND BEYOND

VENUS

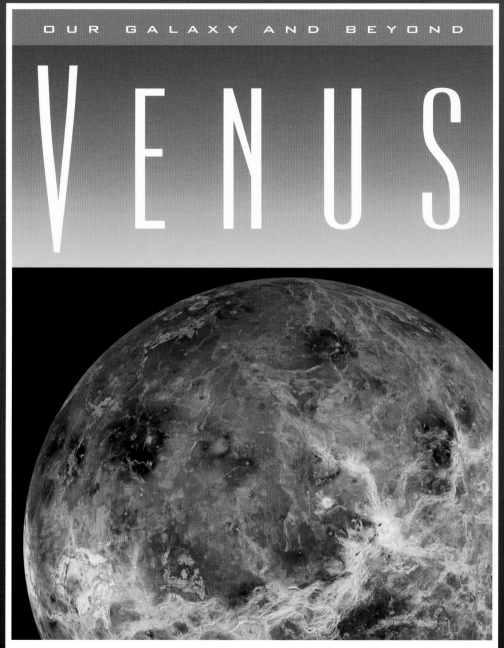

By Charnan Simon

Published in the United States of America by The Child's World®
P.O. Box 326, Chanhassen, MN 55317-0326
800-599-READ
www.childsworld.com

Photo Credits: Cover: NASA/JPL/Caltech; Bettmann/Corbis: 8, 9, 23; Corbis: 10, 14
(Araldo de Luca), 19; NASA/JPL/Caltech: 7 (MIT/USGS), 13, 16, 18, 21, 22 (USGS),
26, 27; Roger Ressmeyer/Corbis: 5 (NASA), 15, 25.

The Child's World®: Mary Berendes, Publishing Director
Editorial Directions, Inc.: E. Russell Primm, Editorial Director; Dana Rau, Line
Editor; Elizabeth K. Martin, Assistant Editor; Olivia Nellums, Editorial Assistant;
Susan Hindman, Copy Editor; Susan Ashley, Proofreader; Kevin Cunningham,
Peter Garnham, Chris Simms, Fact Checkers; Tim Griffin/IndexServ, Indexer;
Cian Loughlin O'Day, Photo Researcher; Linda S. Koutris, Photo Selector

Content Adviser:
Michelle Nichols,
Lead Educator for
Informal Programs,
Adler Planetarium
& Astronomy
Museum, Chicago,
Illinois

Library of Congress Cataloging-in-Publication Data
Simon, Charnan.
  Venus / by Charnan Simon.
     p. cm. — (Our galaxy and beyond)
Includes index.
Contents: Earth's mysterious twin—Hot and heavy—What Venus is made of—
Many volcanoes—The giant greenhouse—How Venus formed.
  ISBN 1-59296-057-X (lib. bdg. : alk. paper)
  1. Venus (Planet)—Juvenile literature. [1. Venus (Planet)] I. Title. II. Series.
  QB621.S56 2004
  523.42—dc21   2003008041

TABLE OF CONTENTS

CHAPTER ONE

4   Discovering Venus

CHAPTER TWO

12   Venus's Atmosphere

CHAPTER THREE

16   What Venus Is Made Of

CHAPTER FOUR

20   Many Volcanoes

CHAPTER FIVE

24   The Giant Greenhouse

CHAPTER SIX

26   How Venus May Have Formed

28   Glossary

28   Did You Know?

29   Fast Facts

30   How to Learn More about Venus

32   Index

DISCOVERING VENUS

Venus shines like a diamond in Earth's sky just before dawn and just after dusk. Except for the Sun and the Moon, it is the brightest object in the sky. For thousands of years, people have admired its beauty and brilliance. It is one of the most studied planets. Even so, Venus remains one of the most mysterious bodies in the solar system.

Venus is the second planet from the Sun and is our solar system's sixth largest planet. It is often called Earth's twin. The two planets are alike in many ways. They were both formed about 4.6 billion years ago. They are nearly the same size and have the same kind of rocky, solid surface.

In other ways, however, Venus is nothing at all like Earth. Venus is unbelievably hot. Temperatures on its surface can reach up to 900°

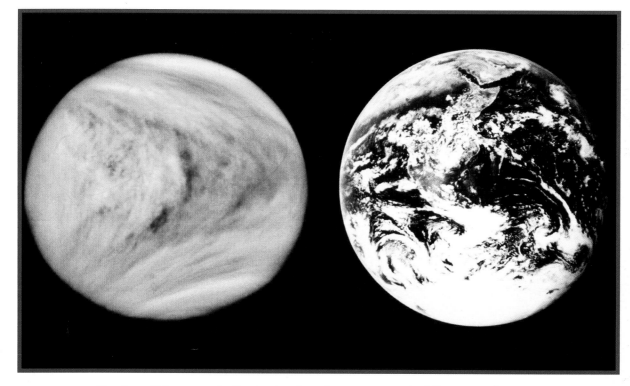

Earth and Venus are similar in size, but they are extremely different in other ways.

Fahrenheit (482° Celsius). This is twice as hot as a very hot oven. The

highest temperature ever recorded on Earth was only 136° F (58° C).

Another difference between Earth and Venus is that Venus has no

liquid water. There may have been large oceans on Venus once, but

they have long since boiled away. There may be some **water vapor**

on Venus, however.

Then, too, Venus is a little, well, backwards. Each of the nine planets in our solar system rotates, or turns, on its axis. An axis is an imaginary line between the top and bottom of a planet, called its north and south poles. Like all the planets except Venus, Earth rotates from west to east. But Venus turns from east to west. What does this mean? On Earth, the Sun rises in the east and sets in the west. If you could stand on Venus, the Sun would appear to rise in the west and set in the east! Venus also rotates very slowly. It takes Earth 24 hours, or one day, to rotate once on its axis. But it takes 243 Earth-days for Venus to rotate once.

Like all the other planets, Venus orbits the Sun in a regular pattern. Earth takes 365 days, or one year, to go around the Sun. Venus is closer to the Sun than Earth is. It moves faster than Earth and has a shorter distance to travel. It only takes Venus 225 Earth-days to

This image of Venus was taken by the Magellan *spacecraft. Both Earth and Venus move around the Sun, but Venus has a shorter distance to travel.*

orbit the Sun. So a year on Venus is shorter than a year on Earth.

But remember—it takes Venus 243 Earth-days to rotate once on its axis. On Venus, a day is longer than a year!

People have been fascinated by Venus for thousands of years. The

Pythagoras was the first person to realize that Venus is not two separate stars.

very earliest **astronomers** thought Venus was two separate stars—a bright star visible in the morning and another bright star visible in the evening. A famous Greek philosopher and mathematician named Pythagoras is said to have been the first person to realize that those two stars were really just the planet Venus.

In the early 1600s, the Italian astronomer Galileo became the first person to see Venus through a **telescope.** Venus seems like an easy planet to study. It is bright and close to Earth. But as Galileo and other astronomers soon found out, studying Venus is harder than it seems. The planet is completely covered by thick clouds. It is impossible to see its surface with regular telescopes.

Galileo saw Venus through a telescope in the early 1600s.

Today, much of what we know about Venus comes from looking through special telescopes, called radio telescopes, here on Earth. Even more information comes from **satellites** orbiting Earth and from space **probes.** The United States and Russia have been sending spacecraft to Venus since the early 1960s. They have gathered volumes of information about our mysterious neighbor in space.

Some of the spacecraft flew past Venus. Others went into orbit around the planet. Some probes crashed into the surface of Venus. A few have even tried to land. But none of these probes has lasted more than a couple of hours because of Venus's terrible heat and the enormous pressure of the planet's atmosphere.

This drawing shows the path of the Magellan *spacecraft as it orbited Venus.*

MAGELLAN SPACECRAFT

On May 4, 1989, the *Magellan* spacecraft was launched from the space shuttle *Atlantis*. Its mission, or purpose, was to map the surface of Venus.

After *Magellan* was released from *Atlantis*'s shuttle bay, it looped around the Sun and went into orbit around Venus. From August 10, 1990, to October 12, 1994, *Magellan* circled the planet. It made detailed maps of 98 percent of Venus's surface.

No ordinary camera can take pictures through Venus's thick clouds. Instead, *Magellan* used radar. Radar, which stands for RAdio Detecting And Ranging, is a type of radio signal. Radar works by sending out a radio signal, or beam. If the beam hits something, it bounces back. On *Magellan*, specially designed antennae aimed radio signals through the clouds to the surface of Venus. These signals bounced off mountains and craters. They measured how high and deep those landforms were. They also measured heat coming from the planet. All these radio signals were then sent back to Earth. Using computers, astronomers could make these radio signals into a maps of Venus's surface.

Magellan's maps were amazing! For the first time, astronomers could clearly tell what Venus looked like. Volcanic domes, enormous valleys, clusters of craters—there was enough information to keep scientists busy for years.

And what happened to *Magellan?* On October 12, 1994, its mission was completed. The spacecraft went out of orbit and crashed into the hot, seething atmosphere of Venus. Its mission was completed.

CHAPTER TWO

VENUS'S ATMOSPHERE

An atmosphere is the layer of gases that surrounds a planet. Earth's atmosphere is mostly nitrogen and oxygen gases, and is just right for us to breathe. The atmosphere on Venus is mostly carbon dioxide. Carbon dioxide is the same gas that makes soda fizzy. It is NOT just right for humans to breathe.

A thick layer of swirling clouds completely covers Venus. These clouds let in the Sun's heat, but they don't let it back out. The heat is trapped, which makes Venus hot. Day and night, year after year, the temperature on Venus reaches almost 900° F (482° C). This is hot enough to melt metals such as tin and lead!

The atmosphere on Venus is also very thick and heavy. This atmosphere weighs down on the planet and creates enormous air pressure.

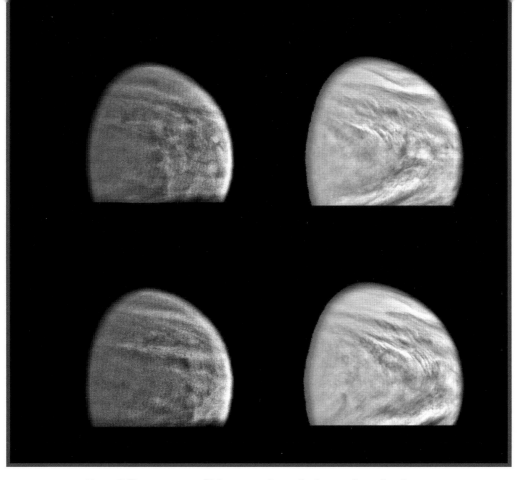

Four different views of Venus, with its thick, swirling cloud cover

In fact, the surface air pressure on Venus is 90 times greater than on Earth. Standing on Venus would be like standing deep, deep under the ocean with all that water pressing down on you. The pressure would be enough to crush a person.

Inside the thick clouds high above Venus is a little bit of water vapor and a gas called sulfur dioxide. When the water vapor mixes

A statue of the Roman goddess Venus

with the sulfur dioxide, it forms droplets of sulfuric acid. Sulfuric acid

is what causes acid rain here on Earth. It is very dangerous to people.

Venus is smothered with a thick, poisonous smog of acid rain.

Venus is named after the Roman goddess of love and beauty. But

it's not exactly a place you'd love to visit!

CLOUDS AND MORE CLOUDS

The planets in our solar system don't shine all by themselves. Only stars, such as the Sun, can do that. Instead, planets shine by reflecting sunlight. This means that sunlight bounces off of them. Venus's clouds are the major reason that the planet shines so brightly. The clouds on Venus reflect 76 percent of the sunlight that strikes the planet. Most other planets reflect much less sunlight. Instead, they soak in, or absorb, the light that hits them.

The clouds on Venus are much higher than the clouds on Earth. They are also much thicker—several miles thick, in fact. These clouds circle the planet about every four days. They are moved along by winds that blow as fast as 217 miles (350 kilometers) per hour. This is faster than most hurricanes on Earth! Daytime on Venus is about as bright as a cloudy day on Earth. The Sun, if it is visible at all, probably looks like an orange smear in the sky.

CHAPTER THREE

What Venus Is Made Of

Like Earth, Venus has a solid iron center, or core, surrounded by a partly liquid outer core. Next comes a mantle made of rocks so hot that they bend and ooze. Covering this mantle is a bumpy, rocky surface called the crust.

The Golubkina crater on the rocky, uneven surface of Venus

On Earth we enjoy mountains and oceans, forests and deserts, grassy plains and rushing rivers. But Venus is mostly a vast, gently rolling desert with many **volcanoes.** It is covered with sand, gravel, dull gray rocks, and lots of lava. Lava is the hot, melted rock that flows from a volcano. The landscape of Venus has been almost entirely shaped by volcanoes and lava. There are lava plains, lava hills, lava rivers, and even large, volcanic mountains.

Scientists think that once, billions of years ago, Venus was dotted with craters. Like the other planets in the solar system, Venus has probably been struck by many **meteorites** during its history. But then, about 300 million to 500 million years ago, the planet's surface seems to have changed. Its old craters were covered with newer volcanic lava flows. Of course, there are still some craters on Venus. But there aren't many small ones. Scientists think that smaller meteors are destroyed by Venus's atmosphere before they can reach the surface.

Venus may once have been more like Earth. It may have contained water. But something happened, and all the water evaporated, or heated up and turned into gas. Today, Venus is dry and lifeless.

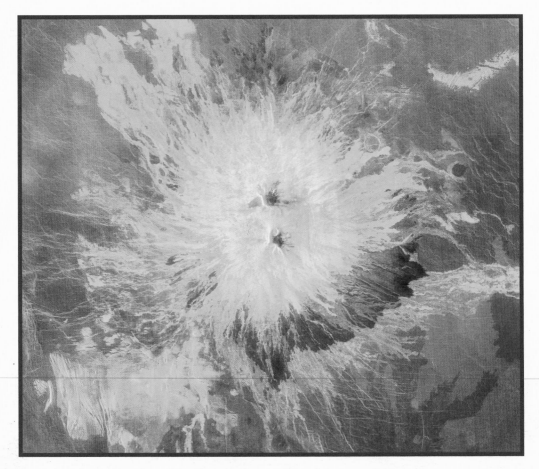

An overhead view of one of Venus's many volcanoes

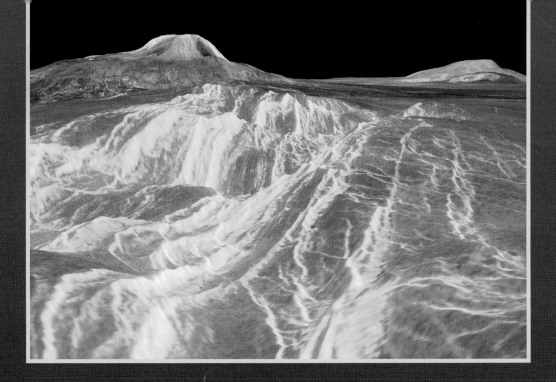

EROSION

Erosion is the process by which rocks and other landforms are gradually worn away. On Earth, wind, water, and ice are all causes of erosion. The main force of erosion is water. Over millions of years, water can wear down the tallest mountain or fill in the deepest basin.

Venus doesn't have much erosion. Even though the winds above the planet are very strong, the winds on the

(1.6 km) per hour. That's not strong enough to wear away rock. And Venus doesn't have any water to change the landscape. The acid in its atmosphere probably eats away at rocks a little, but not much.

Without erosion, nothing changes for long, long periods of time. So even though Venus's volcanoes and lava flows are millions of years old, they still look as if they were

CHAPTER FOUR

MANY VOLCANOES

Volcanoes of all shapes and sizes can be found on Venus. The tallest volcano on Venus is the enormous Maxwell Mons, or Mount Maxwell. Maxwell Mons reaches almost 7 miles (11 km) into the sky. That's much higher than Earth's tallest point, Mount Everest. Maxwell Mons is one of the highest mountains in our solar system. At its top, or summit, is a crater nearly 50 miles (80 km) wide. Scientists don't know if Maxwell Mons is an active volcano. Active volcanoes still erupt. They produce sulfur dioxide. The sulfur dioxide in Venus's atmosphere is a clue that some active volcanoes might still exist. But scientists haven't found any yet.

On Earth, volcanic eruptions are loud, spectacular explosions. Volcanoes are a little different on Venus. Instead of big explosions and huge clouds of ash, volcanoes on Venus mostly just oozed a lot of liquid lava when they erupted.

This lava, now cooled and hardened, is everywhere. In some places, there are huge basins filled with lava. One raised basin, called

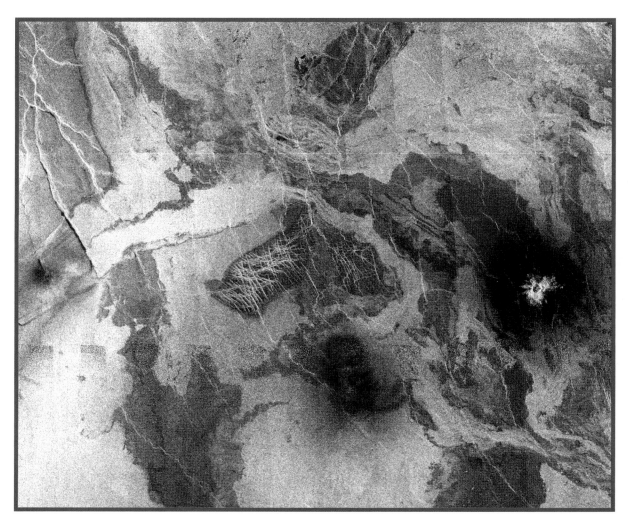

An image of Lakshmi Lake on Venus shows patterns of hardened lava flows.

the Ishtar Terra, is almost as big as the United States! Maxwell Mons lies along the edge of the Ishtar Terra. In other places, great rivers of solid lava snake along the landscape. These lava rivers can run more than 3,000 miles (4,828 km). That is longer than lava rivers on any other planet.

Most volcanoes on Venus look a lot like volcanoes on Earth. They have gentle slopes, rivers of hardened lava flowing down their sides, and a central opening where the lava escaped.

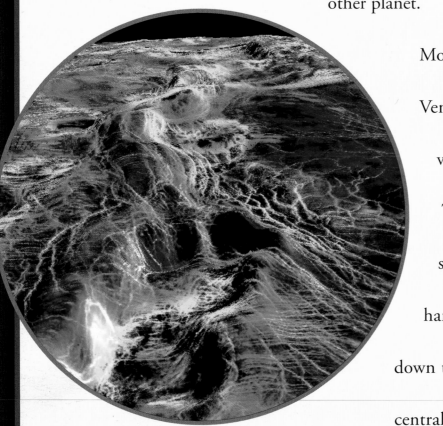

Scientists added extra color to this photograph so that they could study the landscape of Venus. Much of the planet's surface has been shaped by volcanic eruptions.

NAMING THE LANDFORMS OF VENUS

You know that landforms on Earth have names—Mount Everest, the Grand Canyon, the Hawaiian Islands. Landforms on other planets have names, too. The organization responsible for making up these names is the International Astronomical Union (IAU).

When it was time to start naming the mountains, craters, and canyons on Venus, women all over the world wrote to the IAU. Since Venus was the only planet named for a woman, they thought the landforms should be named for women, too. The IAU agreed. Today, all of the physical features on Venus are named either after goddesses from different reli-

The only exception is Maxwell Mons, which is named for James Clerk Maxwell, a 19th-century Scottish physicist. Nahas-tsan Mons, for example, is a mountain named for the Navajo Mother Earth. There are craters named Aglaonice, for an ancient Greek astronomer; Bly, for the 19th-century American journalist Nellie Bly (above); and Heloise, for the 12th-century French doctor. The Chondi Chasma, or Chondi Canyon, is named after the Bengali goddess of wild animals. Seo-Ne Chasma is named for the Korean moon goddess. So far, scientists have found 1,761 features on Venus and named all but one after a

CHAPTER FIVE

THE GIANT GREENHOUSE

Have you ever been in a greenhouse? Greenhouses are warm and steamy even on cold days. The glass walls and roof let in the Sun's rays. But this glass also traps the heat so it can't escape.

Thick clouds of carbon dioxide cover Venus, like the roof of a giant greenhouse. These clouds absorb the Sun's heat and don't let it out again. The trapped heat builds up, and Venus gets hotter and hotter. In fact, Venus is the hottest planet in the solar system. It is even hotter than Mercury, which is much closer to the Sun.

Earth doesn't have nearly as much carbon dioxide in its atmosphere as Venus. Most of this gas is absorbed by our oceans. But scientists are worried about a greenhouse effect here on Earth. The amount of carbon dioxide in Earth's atmosphere is increasing.

Temperatures on Earth are rising, too. Part of this may be due to nature. Part of it is because of the coal and oil that people use as fuel. These fuels create carbon dioxide when they are burned.

Perhaps scientists studying Venus will eventually find a solution to the greenhouse effect on Earth.

This extra carbon dioxide may be trapping more of the Sun's heat and keeping Earth warmer.

What would happen if there were more carbon dioxide than Earth's oceans could absorb? Scientists are studying this problem. Perhaps learning about Venus will help solve the problems of a greenhouse effect here on Earth.

CHAPTER SIX

HOW VENUS
MAY HAVE FORMED

Nearly five billion years ago, a huge cloud of dust and gases

swirled in space. Slowly, our Sun was formed in the center of this

cloud. The Sun used up most of the dust and gas in the huge cloud.

But there was still a lot left over. About 4.6 billion years ago, the

leftovers formed the planets that circle the Sun and make up our

solar system.

*A view of the surface of Venus; this planet was formed
billions of years ago by leftover dust and gas.*

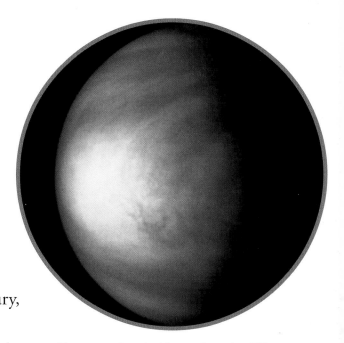

Venus, seen here in blue to show the differences in its clouds, is considered a "terrestrial planet."

Scientists think the swirling cloud was thicker near the Sun. It contained more metals, such as iron and nickel. So the four planets closest to the Sun—Mercury, Venus, Earth, and Mars—are mostly made of rock and metal. They are known as the "terrestrial planets," meaning that they have a solid surface the way Earth does. On the other hand, the outer planets of Jupiter, Saturn, Uranus, and Neptune are called "gas giants" because they are made mostly of gases. No one is really sure what tiny, faraway Pluto is made of.

Astronomers have learned much about Earth's twin since the time of Galileo. But Venus still holds many mysteries that have yet to be answered.

Glossary

astronomers (uh-STRAW-nuh-merz) Astronomers are scientists who study space and the stars and planets.

craters (CRAY-tuhrs) Craters are large, bowl-shaped holes on a planet or moon caused when a comet, asteroid, or meteorite hits its surface.

meteorites (MEE-tee-uh-rites) Meteorites are rocky, metallic objects from space that hit the surface of a planet or moon.

probes (PROBES) Probes are machines or tools that explore something.

radio signal (RAY-dee-oh SIG-nuhl) A radio signal is a magnetic wave formed by electricity that is sent out a certain number of times per second.

satellites (SAH-tuh-lites) Satellites are smaller objects in orbit around a larger object in space and can be man-made or natural. For example, the Moon is a satellite of Earth.

telescope (TEL-uh-skope) A telescope is an instrument used to study things that are far away, such as stars and planets, by making them seem larger and closer.

volcanoes (vol-KAY-nose) Volcanoes are mountains that contain an opening in the surface of a planet. When a volcano erupts, melted rock from pools of magma below the surface spews from the top.

water vapor (WAH-ter VAY-pur) Water vapor is a gas created when water is heated. An example is the steam coming from a teakettle.

Did You Know?

▸ Venus is named after the ancient Roman goddess of love and beauty and is the only planet named after a woman. The Greeks called Venus Aphrodite, after their goddess of love. The Babylonians called it Ishtar, meaning "bright torch of heaven." To the Chinese, Venus was Tai-pe, or "beautiful white one."

▸ Early astronomers thought planets were stars that moved across the sky, while the other stars stood still. The word *planet* comes from the Greek word *planatae,* which means "wanderer."

▶ The U.S. *Mariner 2* spacecraft was the first to fly by Venus in 1962. In 1965, the *Venera 3* from the Soviet Union (now Russia) became the first spacecraft to reach another planet when it crash-landed on Venus. The Soviet *Venera 7* was the first spacecraft to actually soft-land on a planet when it reached Venus in 1970. It was destroyed by heat and pressure in just 23 minutes. More than 20 spacecraft have visited Venus.

▶ Some spacecraft have found evidence of lightning on Venus. Others have not. Scientists are still unsure about whether or not lightning occurs on the planet.

Fast Facts

Diameter: 7,520 miles (12,104 km)

Atmosphere: mostly carbon dioxide, some nitrogen, sulfur dioxide

Time to orbit the Sun (one Venus-year): 225 Earth-days

Time to turn on axis (one Venus-day): 243 Earth-days

Shortest distance from the Sun: 66.8 million miles (107.5 million km)

Greatest distance from the Sun: 67.7 million miles (108.9 million km)

Shortest distance from Earth: 26 million miles (42 million km)

Greatest distance from Earth: 162 million miles (261 million km)

Surface gravity: 0.91 that of Earth. A person weighing 80 pounds (36 kg) on Earth would weigh about 73 pounds (33 kg) on Venus.

Temperature range: 867° F (464° C) on average; it does not change much.

Number of known moons: 0

How to Learn More about Venus

At the Library

Asimov, Isaac, and Richard Hantula. *Venus.* Milwaukee: Gareth Stevens, 2002.

Haugen, David. *Venus.* San Diego: Kidhaven Press, 2002.

Miller, Ron. *Venus.* Brookfield, Conn.: Twenty-First Century Books, 2003.

Spangenburg, Ray. *A Look at Venus.* Danbury, Conn.: Franklin Watts, 2001.

Sparrow, Giles. *Venus.* Chicago: Heinemann Library, 2001.

Stone, Tanya Lee. *Venus.* New York: Benchmark Books, 2002.

On the Web

Visit our home page for lots of links about Venus:
http://www.childsworld.com/links.html
Note to Parents, Teachers, and Librarians: We routinely verify our Web links to
make sure they're safe, active sites—so encourage your readers to check them out!

Through the Mail or by Phone

ADLER PLANETARIUM AND ASTRONOMY MUSEUM
1300 South Lake Shore Drive
Chicago, IL 60605-2403
312/922-STAR

NATIONAL AIR AND SPACE MUSEUM
7th and Independence Avenue, S.W.
Washington, DC 20560
202/357-2700

LUNAR AND PLANETARY INSTITUTE
3600 Bay Area Boulevard
Houston, TX 77058
281/486-2139

The solar system

Index

acid rain, 14
air pressure, 12–13
Algaonice crater, 23
astronomers, 8
Atlantis (shuttle), 11
atmosphere, 9, 10, 12–14, 15, 18, 19, 24
axis, 6

basins, 21–22
Bly crater, 23
Bly, Nellie, 23

carbon dioxide, 12, 24
Chondi Chasma, 23
clouds, 9, 15
core, 16
craters, 11, 17, 23
crust, 16

erosion, 19

formation, 4, 26–27

Galileo, 8
"gas giants," 27

greenhouse effect, 24–25

Heloise crater, 23

International Astronomical Union (IAU), 23
Ishtar Terra basin, 22

lava, 17, 19, 21, 22

Magellan spacecraft, 11
mantle, 16
Maxwell, James Clerk, 23
Maxwell Mons, 20, 23
meteorites, 17
meteors, 18
mountains, 11, 17, 19

Nahas-tsan Mons, 23
names, 14, 23
north pole, 6

orbit, 6–7

poles, 6
probes. *See* spacecraft.

Pythagoras, 8

radar, 11
rotation, 6

satellites, 9
Seo-Ne Chasma, 23
size, 4
solar system, 15, 26
south pole, 6
spacecraft, 9–10
sulfur dioxide, 13–14, 20
Sun, 6, 12, 15, 26
surface, 4, 10, 16, 17, 27

telescopes, 8
temperatures, 4–5, 10, 12, 24
"terrestrial planets," 27

volcanoes, 17, 19, 20–22

water, 5, 18
winds, 15, 19

About the Author

Charnan Simon has a B.A. in English literature from Carleton College and an M.A. in English literature from the University of Chicago. She began her publishing career in Boston, in the children's book division of Little, Brown and Company. She also spent six years as an editor at *Cricket* magazine before becoming a full-time author. Simon has written more than 40 books for kids, and numerous magazine stories and articles. In addition to writing and freelance editing, she is also a contributing editor for *Click* magazine. Simon lives in Madison, Wisconsin, with her husband Tom, their daughters, Ariel and Hana, Sam the dog, and Lily and Luna the cats.